J
599.67
Roy

P9-CEI-051

Bedford Free Public Library
Bedford, Massachusetts 01730

Home of the Bedford Flag

DISCARDED

The Bedford Flag, commissioned to Cornet John
Page in 1737 by King George II of England, was
carried by his son, Nathaniel, who fought with the
Bedford Minutemen at the Battle of Concord
Bridge, April 19, 1775.

OCT   2017

KATHERINE ROY

HOW TO BE AN
ELEPHANT

GROWING UP *in the* AFRICAN WILD

David Macaulay Studio • Roaring Brook Press

New York

WITH FLAPPING EARS and whiffling trunks, the herd quickly spreads the news. After 22 months of growing, a new baby is on her way. From walking and rumbling to drinking and dining, nothing will come easy for this giant-to-be. But like her mother before her, she'll have to *learn* . . .

. . . how to be an elephant.

BUT HOW WILL SHE DO IT?

It starts with the perfect family . . .

FAMILY MATTERS

AFRICAN ELEPHANTS ARE ONE OF the few species on Earth that live in permanent social groups. The family herd—made up of mothers, sisters, cousins, and calves—is usually led by the eldest female, or matriarch. While males leave during adolescence, related females often stay together for life, cooperating to share resources, avoid danger, and care for each other's young. Their extraordinary teamwork and combined experience provide a safe and stable training ground for growing up—a perfect classroom made up of welcoming trunks, available to every newborn baby.

Like a human baby, an elephant calf has to learn nearly everything, an education that begins at birth and lasts for a lifetime. Though she may not need to tie her shoes or ride a bicycle, there are a multitude of skills that are critical to her survival and development that will take days, months, or even years to get right. Her family will support this learning process throughout her long childhood and adolescence, with each member modeling the physical and social behaviors of elephant life around her as she grows. This treasury of knowledge—passed down through the generations—will give her a strong foundation as she begins her journey to adulthood, starting with her first lesson as a brand-new elephant . . .

MADE FOR WALKING

WALKING IS NOT AN EASY TASK FOR a 220-pound newborn, but elephant calves are targets for predators, so a baby is built to be on her feet right from the start. Her skeleton is made of spongy bone tissue that is lightweight but able to bear heavy loads, and the construction of her pillar-like legs gives her body extra stability. A fatty pad inside each heel cushions her foot with every step, absorbing shock and sound while keeping her balanced on her tiptoes. Even the cracks in the soles of her feet provide traction, like the tread on a hiking boot.

This heavy-duty design will enable a baby elephant to walk, swim, kneel, and climb, even when she reaches her adult weight of over 7,000 pounds. (Males can reach 13,000 pounds or more.) She'll be able to hit speeds of up to 24 miles per hour, fast enough to charge at a threatening lion or make a hasty retreat.

A family member's trunk helps the baby find her footing—she totters, falls, then tries again—and she successfully takes her first steps within about an hour of birth. After the baby nurses, the herd resumes its march at a slower pace. To keep track of her mother, the wobbly calf needs her next elephant lesson . . .

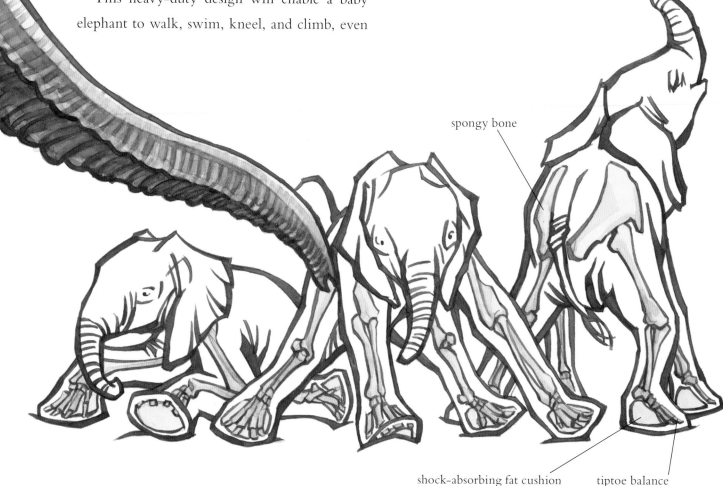

spongy bone

shock-absorbing fat cushion

tiptoe balance

SMELL-O-VISION

WITH EVERY SNIFF, A BABY ELEPHANT samples the air, breathing in the details of an acacia or an aunt. Unlike humans, elephants have poor vision, so a calf partly "sees" the world around her by following her nose. A bouquet of aromas made of tiny odor molecules travels a few feet up her extra-long nasal cavities to land on supersized nasal folds that are covered with highly sensitive receptor cells. These cells send signals to the olfactory bulb in her brain, where they are decoded into data that can be interpreted and committed to memory.

Thanks in part to this enormous nasal surface area combined with the almost 2,000 genes that are dedicated to smell, an elephant's nose is one of the most perceptive on Earth. Using scent alone, a baby elephant will learn to identify individual family members, locate food and water, catch wind of danger, and—one day— select mates. But smelling isn't the only lesson up a baby's nose . . .

nasal cavity

nostrils

aromas

NOSE JOB

PART HAND, PART ARM, PART NOSE, and part shower, an elephant's trunk is perhaps the most multipurpose animal appendage in the world. With over 100,000 muscles crisscrossing its length, it has enough strength to uproot a tree and enough precision to pick a single blade of grass. Thousands of whiskers, called vibrissae, along with specialized cells packed into the two opposing "fingers" at the tip, make a trunk exceptionally sensitive to touch and to vibrations in the ground. This one extraordinary tool helps a baby elephant eat, breathe, smell, scratch, sound, gesture, dig, and drink—though she doesn't actually drink liquid *through* her nose; instead, she will learn to suck water up into her trunk and then pour it down her throat. As an adult, she'll drink 20 to 40 gallons a day this way, but for now she takes a drink by sipping water with her mouth.

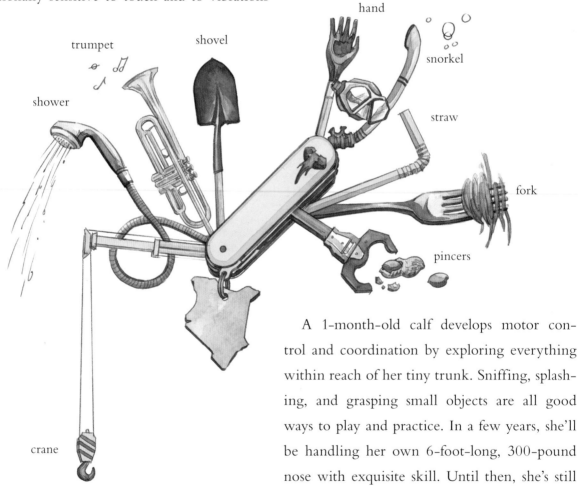

shower · trumpet · shovel · hand · snorkel · straw · fork · pincers · crane

A 1-month-old calf develops motor control and coordination by exploring everything within reach of her tiny trunk. Sniffing, splashing, and grasping small objects are all good ways to play and practice. In a few years, she'll be handling her own 6-foot-long, 300-pound nose with exquisite skill. Until then, she's still in basic training as she soaks up sounds for her next elephant class . . .

SOUND OFF

A BABY ELEPHANT'S VOCABULARY of barks, cries, grunts, and trumpets is designed to call her family's attention to her most basic needs. Like other mammals, elephants make sounds by pushing air out of their lungs and across their vocal cords—causing the cords to vibrate—but with their tremendous body size, elephants get several sound-production upgrades as they age. Larger lungs and bigger sinuses increase amplification, with added resonance from

sinuses

lungs

vocal cords

trachea

vocal tract

ultra-loose vocal cords and a long, flexible vocal tract that can bend to shape tone and pitch. The result is a rich repertoire of call types across a 10-octave range. An adult elephant's voice can reveal her identity and emotional state, escalating to a high-pitched roar at a predator or dropping to a low-frequency rumble signaling that it's time to go. The calf learns how to talk as she listens to the surrounding conversations, ready for a taste of her next elephant lesson . . .

"Let's go" rumble

GUT INSTINCTS

HER MOTHER'S MILK HAS ALL THE nutrition a baby elephant needs before her second birthday, but it takes 300 pounds or more of food a day to run a full-grown adult. To survive in any region or season, elephants have evolved into dietary generalists with digestive systems that can convert all kinds of leaves, grasses, and barks into usable energy. But what the grown-ups gain in menu options, they lose in efficiency—their guts absorb less than 50 percent of the nutrients they take in, so they have to forage for 12 to 18 hours a day just to get enough to eat! This high-fiber diet requires so much continuous grinding that the scientific name for African savanna elephants—*Loxodonta africana*—comes from the diamond-shaped pattern on each of six successive sets of molars.

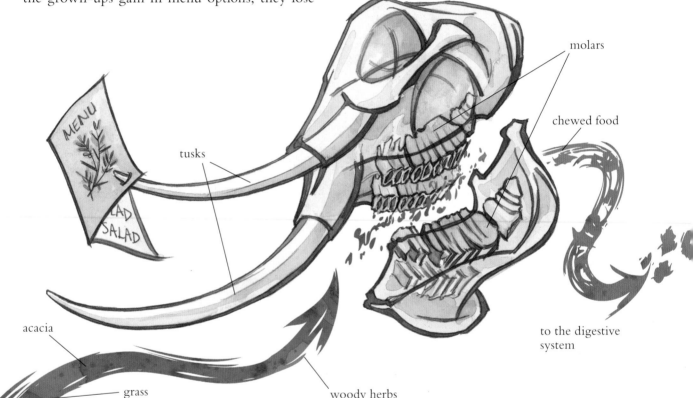

MENU

SALAD

molars

chewed food

tusks

acacia

grass

woody herbs

to the digestive system

forbs (other herbs)

browse

A baby elephant's tusks—which are modified teeth—will appear in about her third year and serve as utensils for slicing grass, stripping bark, and digging for roots and minerals. In the meantime, at 2 months old, it's not too early to learn the local cuisine by stealing samples from any nearby adult's mouth. Food that's already been eaten is also helpful to her developing body—adult elephant dung is full of healthy bacteria and has enough nourishment for a second pass. It's the perfect homemade baby food to savor before warming up for her next skill . . .

CHILL OUT

KEEPING COOL IS A CHALLENGE for any large, round-bodied animal, but African elephants are so enormous that they need several ways to shed extra heat. The moisture trapped in a baby elephant's wrinkled skin cools her down as it evaporates, and her giant ears—the largest in the world—are made for more than just listening. In addition to serving as body fans that can be flapped to create a breeze, her ears are also packed with a network of oversized blood vessels that radiate heat from the blood into the surrounding air with every heartbeat. As a result of these adaptations, an elephant's core body temperature stays at about 97 degrees Fahrenheit on even the hottest days of the year.

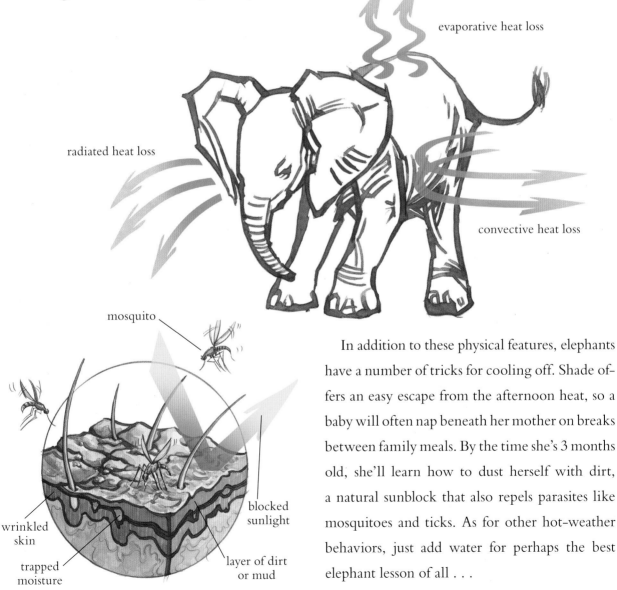

evaporative heat loss

radiated heat loss

convective heat loss

mosquito

wrinkled skin

trapped moisture

blocked sunlight

layer of dirt or mud

In addition to these physical features, elephants have a number of tricks for cooling off. Shade offers an easy escape from the afternoon heat, so a baby will often nap beneath her mother on breaks between family meals. By the time she's 3 months old, she'll learn how to dust herself with dirt, a natural sunblock that also repels parasites like mosquitoes and ticks. As for other hot-weather behaviors, just add water for perhaps the best elephant lesson of all . . .

BUT NOT SO FAST!

EVEN WITH SO MANY LESSONS behind her, a baby elephant still has years of education ahead: where to go, what to say, when to leave, and how to behave around other elephants. Her long-term survival depends upon her ability to learn and to put new lessons into practice within her greater social group and in the world at large.

Playtime is particularly important for a calf, an ongoing rehearsal for how to be an adult.

One favorite elephant game is chasing away "enemy" invaders in boisterous mock battles that are launched at smaller neighborhood species like egrets, baboons, and warthogs. Ears spread, trunk swinging, the young elephant auditions her anti-predator moves. Soon enough, she'll be grown and ready to join her family in confronting more formidable foes . . .

3 years old

6 months old

9 years old

16 years old

Out on the savanna the elephants rumble, forever on the move in search of food, water, and safety. They march in concert with other family herds, tracking one another by the sounds of their voices . . .

GOOD VIBRATIONS

REMEMBER THE LOUD, low-frequency calls that an elephant makes with her high-powered voice? These rumbles fall below the range of human hearing and can travel much farther than higher-frequency sounds—up to 2 miles during the day and over 6 miles at night, when the air is cool. Other elephants within range can hear the rumbles as either sound waves in the air or vibrations in the ground, which they're able to detect with the tips of their trunks and the cushioned soles of their feet.

Low-Frequency Rumbles
(10–35 Hz)

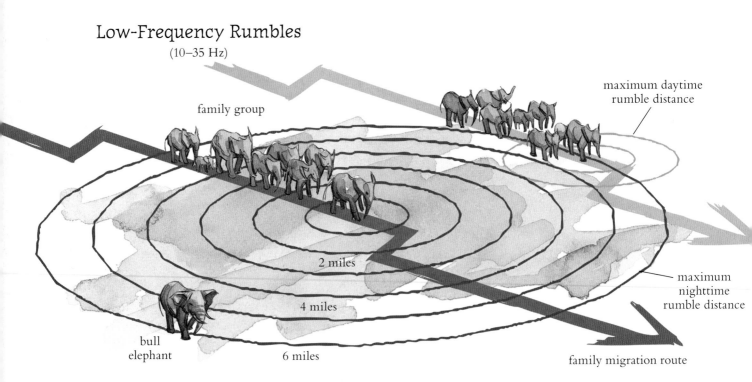

family group

maximum daytime rumble distance

maximum nighttime rumble distance

2 miles

4 miles

bull elephant

6 miles

family migration route

Family members send and receive these long-range broadcasts to stay in touch when they're out of each other's sight and to coordinate their movements with related family groups. Herds merge to eat together when food is abundant and separate to avoid crossing paths during droughts, following familiar routes while sharing information on the whereabouts of predators or potential mates. This "fission-fusion" society, in which relatives frequently split up and regroup, is built on an elephant's ability to recognize and remember the calls of other individuals from afar. The older she gets, the more elephants she'll know, which will strengthen her family's collective social knowledge and help ensure their survival through season after season of change.

MAKING SPACE

AFRICA IS NOT AN EASY PLACE TO live, even for a family of giants. The landscape can shift dramatically from year to year—even week to week! Natural disturbances like fires, droughts, and rainfall can turn forest into grassland or grassland into forest, so elephants must often travel hundreds or even thousands of miles a year to satisfy their huge appetites in such a dynamic home.

Elephants themselves are also agents of change. They strip bark, uproot trees, dig waterholes, and trample the ground, spreading billions

breaking branches

stripping bark

scattering seeds

of seeds as they walk and eat. Passage through an elephant's gut can speed up a seed's germination, and dung piles supply new plants with moisture, nutrients, and physical protection as they grow. Many birds, mammals, and reptiles pick through elephant dung for minerals, insects, and secondhand meals. This wide-ranging cycle of destruction and renewal makes elephants a "keystone" species, meaning that just one herd—even just one individual—impacts the living spaces of many other animal communities.

acacia woodlands

Savanna Ecosystem

fertilizing soil

acacia seedling

spreading seeds through dung

digging roots

trampling ground

COMMON GROUND

THE BODY SIZE OF AN ANIMAL determines two things: how much food it needs to eat, and how much space it takes to meet that need. A mouse eats very little, so it can live in close quarters with many other mice, while an elephant eats a lot, so it needs a great deal of individual habitat.

In the space needed to support just 1 African elephant (about 5 square kilometers), there are also many, many other mammals: on average, 2 hippos, 5 Grevy's zebras, 25 impalas, 48 olive baboons, 164 vervet monkeys, and 10,000 African spiny mice—just to name a few. While most species on the savanna are relatively small, their big numbers add up to a big impact as a group, each one shaping and maintaining their shared ecosystem with every single meal.

5 Square Kilometers

Thomson's gazelle

greater kudu

black rhinoceros

hippopotamus

Like elephants, humans need a lot of space, but our species isn't good at sharing common ground. As the human population expands, elephants face an increasingly fractured landscape, a patchwork of villages, farms, and ranches crisscrossed by fences and busy roads. By saving space for elephants, we save space for the future generations of so many other species too, ensuring that each cycle has the chance to start anew.

vervet
monkey

reticulated
giraffe

gemsbok

African
elephant

leopard

spotted hyena

eland oryx

Grevy's zebra

cape buffalo

honey badger

olive
baboon

impala

wild dog

lion

waterbuck

plains zebra

warthog

cheetah

African spiny
mouse

With open mouths and roaring voices, the herd
quickly spreads the news. In 22 months, a new baby
will be on his way. From sounding and sparring to courting
and guarding, nothing will come easy for this giant-to-be.
But like his father before him, he'll have to *learn* . . .

. . . how to be an elephant.

A NOTE FROM THE AUTHOR

They are born wearing wrinkles. They are friendly, but also fierce. They talk in deafening rumbles, and move around on soundless feet. Their noses have fingers, and they wave hello with their ears. They are wild, majestic, unmistakably marvelous, and—in many ways—so much like us.

My interest in elephants began when I was little, with a few basic facts and a couple of plush toys. As my knowledge grew, so did my fascination, and in May 2014 I went to central Kenya to spend several days with elephant experts in the field, followed by a 10-day safari through other parks and reserves. During my trip, I watched hundreds of elephants while they ate and drank and went about their lives, from playful calves and foraging mothers to huge, lumbering bulls seeking out potential mates. Herds gathered at sunset to drink from the river. A protective matriarch bluff-charged our jeep. Researchers taught me how to identify individuals by the shapes and conditions of their ears and tusks. I met muddy calves at Sheldrick Orphan's Project, and in Samburu National Reserve I witnessed the darting and collaring of a massive 40-year-old bull. I saw families grazing at the base of Kilimanjaro, and sketched the elephants of the Tsavo West and East National Parks, where the iron-rich soil paints their skin a vibrant red. Day after day, I was filled with wonder at their behavior and biology, their sensitivity and strength. But the trip was also a powerful reminder of how fragile and fleeting this species might be.

In Kenya and many other African countries, elephant populations are running out of time. Infrastructure development has increased the rate of human-elephant conflict by compressing herds into less and less space while poachers—fueled by poverty and the global demand for ivory—target the largest elephants with the heaviest tusks. In 1979, there were about 1.3 million elephants in Africa, but in 2016 the Great Elephant Census showed that approximately 350,000 remain. The death of a single elephant can shatter a family's leadership or weaken the gene pool for generations to come, and scientists estimate that at the current rate of decline, African elephants will be gone in 50 years or less. Better land-use practices can go a long way toward ensuring our mutual existence, but ultimately, elephant conservation is a choice. Their most dangerous threat is also the source of their only hope. There's enough space for us all. Are we willing to share it?

SELECTED SOURCES

In addition to my research on the ground in Kenya, I consumed hundreds of books, articles, newsletters, websites, and documentaries while writing and drawing this story. *The Amboseli Elephants*, edited by Cynthia J. Moss, Harvey Croze, and Phyllis C. Lee, and the website ElephantVoices.org, co-founded by Joyce Poole and Petter Granli, are both outstanding resources for a comprehensive look at African elephants in the wild. In addition, the following sources were endlessly helpful; for a full list, please visit my website, katherineroy.com.

SCIENTIFIC ARTICLES

Campos-Arceiz, A., and S. Blake. "Megagardeners of the Forest—The Role of Elephants in Seed Dispersal." *Acta Oecologica*, vol. 37, no. 6, 2011, pp. 542–553.

Damuth, J. "Population Density and Body Size in Mammals." *Nature*, vol. 290, 1981, pp. 699–700.

Garstang, M. "Elephant Infrasounds: Long-Range Communication." *Handbook of Mammalian Vocalization*. Academic Press, 2010, pp. 57–67.

Kowalski, N. L., R. H. Dale, and C. L. Mazur. "A Survey of the Management and Development of Captive African Elephant (*Loxodonta africana*) Calves: Birth to Three Months of Age." *Zoo Biology*, vol. 29, no. 2, 2010, pp. 104–119.

Schulte, B. A., K. Bagley, M. Correll, A. Gray, S. M. Heineman, H. Loizi, M. Malament, N. L. Scott, B. E. Slade, L. Stanley, T. E. Goodwin, and L. E. L. Rasmussen. "Assessing Chemical Communication in Elephants." *Chemical Signals in Vertebrates 10*. Springer, 2006, pp. 140–151.

Stoeger, A. S., and S. de Silva. "African and Asian Elephant Vocal Communication: A Cross-Species Comparison." *Biocommunication of Animals*. Springer, 2014, pp. 21–39.

FURTHER READING & RESOURCES

BOOKS

Downer, A. *Elephant Talk: The Surprising Science of Elephant Communication*. Twenty-First Century Books, 2011.

Kingdon, J., D. Happold, M. Hoffmann, T. Butynski, M. Happold, and J. Kalina, eds. *Mammals of Africa. Volume I: Introductory Chapters and Afrotheria*. Bloomsbury, 2013.

Moss, C. J., H. Croze, and P. C. Lee. *The Amboseli Elephants: A Long-Term Perspective on a Long-Lived Mammal*. University of Chicago Press, 2011.

O'Connell, C., and D. M. Jackson. *The Elephant Scientist*. Houghton Mifflin, 2011.

FILMS

Elephants: Spy in the Herd. John Downer Productions, 2003.

In the Womb: Animals, season 1, episode 2. National Geographic, 2005.

The Secret Life of Elephants, three episodes. BBC Bristol Productions, Animal Planet, and National Geographic, 2009.

WEBSITES

David Sheldrick Wildlife Trust: sheldrickwildlifetrust.org
ElephantVoices: elephantvoices.org
Save the Elephants: savetheelephants.org

ACKNOWLEDGMENTS

Asante is the Swahili word for thank you. I could say it a thousand times and still be unable to fully express my gratitude to the many friends and acquaintances who helped make these pages possible. To my agent, Stephen Barr, for his sustaining curiosity; to my editor, Simon Boughton, for his ongoing faith and patience; to my mentor, David Macaulay, for his relentless support; and to my incredible team at Macmillan, including Andrew Arnold, Roberta Pressel, Anne Diebel, and Mary Van Akin.

To the scientists and researchers who invested in this project, starting with Jake Goheen, whose enthusiasm for mammal biology is matched only by his pragmatism and humor, for so graciously paving my way to Kenya; to Rob Swihart, for his optimism, and for introducing me to Jake—how could I have guessed that a chat on a flight could result in a picture-book research trip? To Sandy Oduor, for his expert driving and thoughtful explanations; to Deborah Boro, Margaret Kinnaird, and the staff at the Mpala Research Center, for their kindness and hospitality; to David Daballen, who must have conspired with the gods to conjure my breathtaking introduction to wild African elephants, and for his warmth, generosity, and insight; to Yiwei Wang, Frank Pope, Lucy King, and the staff at Save the Elephants for their help and welcoming reception; and to Greg Carr, Gina and Bob Poole, Joyce Poole, Fred Bercovitch, Bruce Schulte, Bob Dale, Angela Stoeger, and Joseph Soltis, for their suggestions, resources, and feedback as the manuscript took shape. Thanks also to Odyssey Safaris for my safe passage to the research camps; to Bernard Mwai at Lion Trails Safaris for an unforgettable journey; and to Ben Gitari, safari guide extraordinaire, whose passion for helping others is a gift to everyone he meets.

To Christen Dobson, Xander Warhorse, Jacqueline Podel, Brian Gaisford, Julie DeNeve, Charles Christy, Michael Fairchild, Sara Frazier, and Paul and Kathy Sidenblad for their advice on traveling in Africa; to my mother, who flew almost halfway around the world to join me on safari, for her love and companionship; to Brian Futterman, Lisa Woodward, Kristi Schramm, Karen Shaw, Brie Spells, R. Kikuo Johnson, Michael Sherman, and Laura Terry for their contributions and counsel; and to Jeff Fisher, 1955–2014, who I hope will haunt my studio for the rest of my days.

Lastly, to my husband, Tim Stout, without whom this book would not exist, and who surely deserves a medal for his love and endurance; and to my son, Jackson, who has brightened my life with his joy and who kicked his way through the making of nearly every piece of art in this book. At the outset, I didn't expect this story to intersect with my own so precisely, but for the gift of learning how to be a mom, this book is for the two of them. *Asante, asante, asante.*

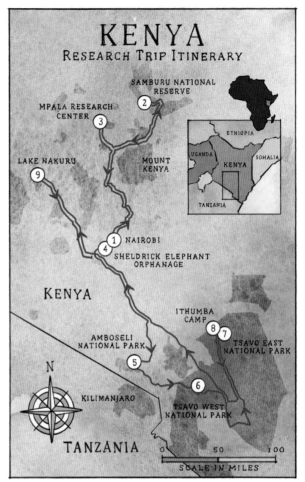

Copyright © 2017 by Katherine Roy
Published by David Macaulay Studio, an imprint of Roaring Brook Press
Roaring Brook Press is a division of Holtzbrinck Publishing Holdings Limited Partnership
175 Fifth Avenue, New York, NY 10010
mackids.com

All rights reserved

Library of Congress Control Number: 2016047511
ISBN 978-1-62672-178-4

Our books may be purchased in bulk for promotional, educational, or business use. Please contact your local bookseller or the Macmillan Corporate and Premium Sales Department at (800) 221-7945 ext. 5442 or by e-mail at MacmillanSpecialMarkets@macmillan.com.

First edition, 2017
Book design by Andrew Arnold
Author photograph by Brian Futterman
Color separations by Bright Arts (H.K.) Ltd.
Printed in China by Toppan Leefung Printing Ltd., Dongguan City, Guangdong Province

1 2 3 4 5 6 7 8 9 10